Made in God's Image Series
Book 3

Identity

Restored | Revealed | Initiate

Discipleship Bible Study
Manual for Christians

C. Orville McLeish

Made in God's Image Series | Book 3. Copyright © 2019. C. Orville McLeish

All rights reserved. No portion of this book may be reproduced, stored in a retrieval system, or transmitted in any form or by any means – electronic, mechanical, photocopy, recording, scanning, or other – except for a brief quotation in critical reviews or articles, without the prior written permission of the publisher or author.

Published by:

HCP BOOK PUBLISHING
www.hcpbookpublishing.com

ISBN: 978-1-949343-51-9 (paperback)

ISBN: 978-1-949343-52-6 (eBook)

Scripture taken from the New King James Version®. Copyright © 1982 by Thomas Nelson. Used by permission. All rights reserved.

Table of Contents

Introduction   1

Chapter One
Restoration of Sight: We Can See   11

    You Are A New Creature   13
    You Are Seated With Christ
       In Heaven   13
    You Are Blessed Beyond Measure   14
    You Lack Nothing   15
    You Have Holy Spirit   15
    Initiate | Engage | Activate   20

Chapter Two
New Living Soul:
Unlimited Possibilities   27

    Initiate | Engage | Activate   37

Chapter Three
Good and Evil: The Battle Within   **41**
     Initiate | Engage | Activate   49

Chapter Four
Redeeming The Imagination:
Renewing Our Minds   **53**
     Initiate | Engage | Activate   64

Chapter Five
All Things Are Yours:
But You Need To Grow Up   **69**
     Initiate | Engage | Activate   78

Conclusion   89

Introduction

I wish I had a resource like this when I just became a believer in Jesus. I had no idea who I was then and for many years to come. One day, someone asked me what my identity in Christ was, and I was unable to answer. I had no clue what that meant or the significance of such a position, but now I do, and this knowledge goes way beyond indoctrination or just trying, in our own strength, to live a holy life. What God has done for humanity is a gift, and whatever service we offer back to Him is out of a heart of gratitude, and nothing else because no "works" can qualify us to receive anything from God.

This Bible Study Series is Christ-centered, You-centered and Biblical as we examine Our Identity in Christ. I recognize that the world is suffering greatly because of an identity crisis. Notice I said the world, and not just Christendom. God made MAN in His OWN IMAGE and likeness, which means God values and loves humanity and not just those who go to church. This identity crisis is the cause of much of the suffering we are experiencing on earth, and I believe if we can change our perception about who we are and begin to walk in (initiate) that reality, the world will subsequently change as well. A re-occurring statement that I hear when I mention certain things is that we don't know who we are. The question is, do we want to? Does not knowing who we are affect how we function as a human being?

I love watching superhero movies because I have been a fan since childhood. There is something to learn from these movies. What we find is that a superhero can have all the powers in the world synonymous with who they are, but function way below their potential because they don't know who they are. In a society like ours where obeah men (witchcraft) seem to have more power than the church, it is a sad reality that most churches will not even admit to that or contemplate why this is so.

My general theme for most of what I write and study about is "Made in God's Image." It is an idea…a thought…an unfolding revelation that takes me deeper into the mind of God. What was God thinking when He made us? How did we look initially? How did we function? What was our super-power? If we were made in God's image, I assume we must have been God-like before the fall. If this is true, and Jesus came to restore all that was lost or redeem what was fallen, then who we were before the fall must be who we are now in Christ, or, at the very least, who we are becoming.

If we should consider a human being before the fall, we can look at Jesus. He was God made flesh who dwelt among us as a man…a sinless man. He is the context we can examine as an example of the possibility of what we were like before the fall. It makes sense because Paul says He is the one we should look at until we are conformed to His image. That word 'conform' is a powerful word, which suggest a transformation into that which we gaze at until one cannot tell the difference between the object of our gaze, and the one who is looking.

If we are becoming like Jesus from faith to faith, and from glory to glory, then at the very basic level we should be able to do the same things He did…not venturing out just yet into the "greater things" He spoke about. We must master the elementary stuff before we can attempt the more complex ideas. Our inability to even do what Jesus did, just to be clear: heal the sick, raise the dead, walk on water, walk through walls, conquer fear and death…speaks to just how far we are from the mark. The question is, how do we move from where we are in our present reality to that Christlikeness and assume our true form and function as a child of God.

I recognize that this may not be for everybody, but if you can relate to anything I am saying so far, then maybe God is speaking to you at a deeper level, and this is for you.

The best place to start in understanding our identity is at the beginning…at our origin, so to speak. Before Genesis 1:1, eternity existed. We say Revelation is a prophetic book, so we put the events of that book somewhere in the future. We also believe that the last verse in revelation is where time ceases to exist, and eternity begins. In that context, eternity also begins for somebody the moment they die. But that is not where eternity begins. Eternity is infinite and cannot be measured. Time is a small space that was made inside eternity for a purpose we might not even be aware of yet. In order to understand who we are, we need to stop thinking of ourselves in the context of beginning and end. Beginning and End is not an event, but a Person, according to Revelation.

Before Genesis, God existed. He is the self-existent One and the One responsible for reality - known and unknown. Never assume that you know it all. A finite mind cannot comprehend infinity. We know in part because that is as much as we can handle now, and there is no one human being or denomination that has the complete truth. Even the occultic movements have a piece of the truth.

So, let me be controversial for a moment. It seems like a terrible assumption to make that God, the Creator, did nothing before Genesis 1:1. I have heard it said that God created many worlds before our own. Why wouldn't that be true? If God exists in a reality that cannot be measured, then there are possibilities we cannot begin to fathom.

God is limitless and He fills up space without limits. If the universe is ever expanding, as our scientific minds have concluded, then God would appear to be unknowable, unless He choose to make Himself known. One of the ways He choose to make Himself known is by creating you. We have a better chance at knowing ourselves. I believe that in knowing our true self, we come into some knowledge of who the Father is because He made us according to His image and likeness. We are only ever aware of our immediate, physical surrounding, and most of us don't even look up at the stars anymore, which I believe is a good practice in stretching our mind to accept that there must be more to life than our immediate physical reality.

Genesis 1:1 says "In the beginning…" Which is a location identified; a little slit in eternity that serves as the starting point for our entrance into this created world. Our world…that the Father built for us.

Did we exist in another form before Adam was created? I don't know. With God, anything is possible.

So, God made the heavens and the earth, then He said, "Let us make man." He formed man and breathe life into man and man became a living soul; not a living body (as we often consider ourselves) and not a living spirit. What did a living soul look like? How did we function? What were we able to do? What was God's intention for man? How did the fall change us?

This series will provide some answers of my own to these questions, but it was designed to provoke thought, study and a deeper desire to know God and who you are in God. For every question we answer, twenty new questions take its place. It will take eternity for us to begin to fathom the depths of God, so our identity in Him is an ever-unfolding revelation. I want you to be open to new revelations from the Holy Spirit as you traverse through the content of this study. Pay close attention to the sections at the end of each Chapter titled: Initiate | Engage | Activate. If you do not Initiate what has been Restored and Revealed, it will not become your reality. Study and Practice is the key to transformation.

> **Study and Practice is the key to transformation.**

Everyone seems to have their own idea about who God is; what He is doing today; how He acts; the things He will and will not do. But we have it backwards. We are God's idea. What He thinks about us is far more valuable, and far more true than what we think about Him.

So, if this sounds like a journey you want to take with me, go ahead and proceed through the next chapters. A video series for this book will also be available on our YouTube Channel:

https://www.youtube.com/channel/UCBb5uZEy77jrIS3ZoUNsjEw

Be sure to subscribe so you will be notified when a new teaching and/or resource is posted. I look forward to our time together.

Shalom.

CHAPTER ONE

Restoration of Sight: We Can See

Where do we begin in knowing our identity in Christ? We can start with the present, then go back to the beginning and work our way back to the present. By the time we get back to this present point, you should be able to look at yourself differently.

Let's talk about the salvation experience. Let's begin there. What happens when we say yes to Jesus?

The Bible says if anyone is in Christ, he is a new creature. The old is passed away - the new has come (See 2 Corinthians 5:17). From this we can say that there is an old version of us that became redundant, and something new took its place. We became new, somehow, when we got saved.

Some argue that the new you is spirit, others say it is the soul. Personally, I agree with the theory of the soul being new, but, either way, this new version of us comes as a baby.

There is a process of maturity that every believer needs to go through, in a similar way that a baby grows into an adult. The reality is, the mature adult that you become existed fully in potential within you as a baby. You just needed to go through the process to unlock the fullness of who you were meant to become. Likewise, the process of a believer in Christ. Christianity is the process of us becoming the image and likeness of God.

> **Christianity is the process of us becoming the image and likeness of God.**

What we want to talk about is what exist in you fully in potential because your identity is tied to that. So what happens when we said yes to Jesus? A couple things, according to Scripture.

You Are A New Creature

> *Therefore, if anyone is in Christ, he is a new creation; old things have passed away; behold, all things have become new.* (2 Corinthians 5:17).

You become a new, living soul, as Adam and Eve were before the fall. You are a new being.

You Are Seated With Christ In Heaven

> *But God, who is rich in mercy, because of His great love with which He loved us, even when we were dead in trespasses, made us alive together with Christ (by grace you have been saved), and raised us up together, and made us sit together in the heavenly places in Christ Jesus, that in the <u>ages to come</u> He might show the exceeding riches of His grace in His kindness toward us in Christ Jesus. For by grace you have been saved through faith, and that not of*

> *yourselves; it is the gift of God, not of works, lest anyone should boast. For we are His workmanship, created in Christ Jesus for good works, which God prepared beforehand that we should walk in them.*
> (Ephesians 2:4-10).

Note carefully: We are in the ages to come; and there are possibly more ages to come.

Note as well: Jesus prayed in John 14:3 that where He is, we may be also.

We are already with Jesus, which is why I don't buy into the version of Christianity that says we need to work our way into heaven or earn our seat there. It is not by works, so no man can boast. Your position in heaven is secured the moment you said yes to Jesus because you are there.

You Are Blessed Beyond Measure

> *Blessed be the God and Father of our Lord Jesus Christ, who has blessed us with every*

> *spiritual blessing in the heavenly places in Christ.*
>
> (Ephesians 1:3).

You Lack Nothing

> *Grace and peace be multiplied to you in the knowledge of God and of Jesus our Lord, as His divine power has given to us all things that pertain to life and godliness, through the knowledge of Him who called us by glory and virtue, by which have been given to us exceedingly great and precious promises, that through these you may be partakers of the divine nature, having escaped the corruption that is in the world through lust.*
>
> (2 Peter 1:2-4).

You Have Holy Spirit

> *Or do you not know that your body is the temple of the Holy Spirit who is in you,*

> *whom you have from God, and you are not your own? For you were bought at a price; therefore glorify God in your body and in your spirit, which are God's.*
>
> (1 Corinthians 6:19-20).

Holy Spirit is given freely to everyone who confesses Jesus as Lord.

> *But you shall receive power when the Holy Spirit has come upon you; and you shall be witnesses to Me in Jerusalem, and in all Judea and Samaria, and to the end of the earth.*
>
> (Acts 1:8).

You can receive the baptism of the Holy Spirit by asking:

> *If you then, being evil, know how to give good gifts to your children, how much more will your heavenly Father give the Holy Spirit to those who ask Him.*
>
> (Luke 11:13).

The moment you ask for the Holy Spirit, you receive Him from God. That is a promise and God will always honor His word. Even if you don't speak in tongues, you have received Holy Spirit. Most of the times you don't speak because of fear and uncertainty, and not because you have not received.

These are at least five things that come in the salvation package. These five apply to all of us as believers in Christ, at the very least, in potential, but as you grow up, additional levels or dimensions of each of these will unlock in your life.

Salvation puts us in Christ, in God. We become partakers of His nature and His identity. The process of maturity is to conform to our new position. I need you to understand that before we talk about the beginning. Read it repeatedly and memorize it, because it speaks to who you are now.

So, let's go now to the beginning.

I could start with Genesis 1:1, but I have a better idea. Let's start with the prophet who wrote the first five books of the Bible, or what we call the Torah. His name is Moses.

Keep in mind that we are talking about our identity in God, in Christ.

Moses had a solid relationship with God; face to face. Most of us want that.

So, he is standing with God on a mountain; or in another dimension; whatever the case may be, and he makes a request. "Lord, show me your glory."

God says, "I can't show you my face" in that moment for whatever reason, because we know the Bible said God talked to Moses face to face, mouth to mouth.

God says, there is a place near me where I can put you. I will cover you in the cleft of the rock. (See Exodus 33:18-23).

Now we have this song we sing that says, "This rock is Jesus, yes He's the one." The Bible also says Jesus is the rock (See 1 Corinthians 10:4).

If Jesus is the rock that was by God's side, and God put Moses in Jesus, isn't it possible that Moses was able to see all that God did in detail from the beginning of time up to that present moment?

God showed Moses what was behind Him (God) not what was in front of Him.

The question with Moses being the author of the Torah is, how did he write about his own death in Deuteronomy 34. I am thinking he saw the whole thing, even his death (and when I talk about death, it is relative, because we don't really die; we sleep - because we see Moses appearing to Jesus on the mount of transfiguration, so we really need to develop some new doctrines about this "death" thing).

Moses saw in profound details the hand of God in creation. So, now he says, "In the beginning, God -" Moses is the one who wrote that, because I believe he saw it.

In the beginning could span thousands or millions of years; or it could be a day. Whatever the case may be, Jesus was there. The Bible says in John 1:1, "In the beginning " - same term - was the Word and the Word was with God and the Word was God. John wrote that. I believe he saw it.

The Holy Spirit was also there in the beginning. If the Holy Spirit was indeed there, hovering over the waters, bringing order from chaos by the Word of God, and He was there, in eternity before that, and He now lives inside you, then the history of God Himself in creation is sitting inside the believer, and you have access to all that.

So, here's the thing:

In Christ, you are able to see the past (even long before you were born in this realm) and you are also able to see the future because sight has been restored.

Initiate | Engage | Activate
Meditation Scriptures:

> *Blessed are the pure in heart, for they shall see God.*
>
> (Matthew 5:8).

By faith Moses, when he became of age, refused to be called the son of Pharaoh's daughter, choosing rather to suffer affliction with the people of God than to enjoy the passing pleasures of sin, esteeming the reproach of Christ greater riches than the treasures in Egypt; for he looked to the reward. By faith he forsook Egypt, not fearing the wrath of the king; for he endured as seeing Him who is invisible.
(Hebrews 11:24-27).

Jesus answered and said to him, "Most assuredly, I say to you, unless one is born again, he cannot see the kingdom of God."
(John 3:3).

Therefore I also, after I heard of your faith in the Lord Jesus and your love for all the saints, do not cease to give thanks for you, making mention of you in my prayers: that the God of our Lord Jesus Christ, the Father of glory, may give to you the spirit of wisdom and revelation in the knowledge of Him, the eyes of your understanding being enlightened; that you may know what is the hope of His calling, what are the riches of the glory of His inheritance in the saints, and what is the exceeding greatness of His power toward us who believe, according to the working of His mighty power.

(Ephesians 1:15-19).

But from there you will seek the Lord your God, and you will find Him if you seek Him with all your heart and with all your soul.

(Deuteronomy 4:29).

For it is the God who commanded light to shine out of darkness, who has shone in our hearts to give the light of the knowledge of the glory of God in the face of Jesus Christ.

(2 Corinthians 4:6).

The utterance of him who hears the words of God, who sees the vision of the Almighty, who falls down, with eyes wide open.

(Numbers 24:4).

> *And Elisha prayed, and said, "Lord, I pray, open his eyes that he may see." Then the Lord opened the eyes of the young man, and he saw. And behold, the mountain was full of horses and chariots of fire all around Elisha.*
> *(2 Kings 6:17).*
>
> *Then their eyes were opened and they knew Him; and He vanished from their sight.*
> *(Luke 24:31).*
>
> *For you were once darkness, but now you are light in the Lord. Walk as children of light.*
> *(Ephesians 5:8).*

The process of seeing can be a long one that demands a lot of consistent perseverance and intentional "pressing in."

Close your eyes for five minutes. Try not to think any thoughts, just observe; just look.

What do you see?

The most common answer to that question is "nothing." But we actually saw something;

we saw darkness, which means we saw something.

Some of the leading Christian Mystics of this age suggest that we are seeing darkness because we have no reference for what we are looking at. It is the same for a baby born into this world. Their eyes are wide open, but they really do not know what they are looking at. We are the ones who teach them, and the more they learn, is the more their world expands.

We have a Teacher, Holy Spirit, who knows what we are looking at, and we must learn to engage Him in the process. We must ask questions, as a child would, and listen for the response. He will teach us how to see, and the more we see, the more the real world will begin to expand.

So, meditate in silence for as long as you can, daily, look at the darkness until you feel it expanding, ask the Holy Spirit questions and listen for the answer. The Holy Spirit is there (in you and on you), and you can begin to develop that relationship with Him and allow Him to become a part of your reasoning process. Allow the Holy Spirit to teach you how to see.

CHAPTER TWO

New Living Soul: Unlimited Possibilities

I believe Moses saw and wrote enough for us to begin to understand who we really are in God. I want you to remember something; keep this at the front of your mind: You are God's idea; How He made you to function; the identity He gave you; your nature and potential as a human being, it was all His idea, not yours. God is the only One who can tell us who we are (Ref. Isaiah 45:18-24).

> God is the only One who can tell us who we are (Ref. Isaiah 45:18-24).

So, let's look at what it really means to be human.

Now, notice a trend in the story of creation. God created the sea, then the fish; He created the lands, then the animals; He created the sky, then the birds. So, before the living creature, the habitat had to be established that this creature lives in.

The suggestion here is that God made the heavens and the earth mentioned in Genesis 1 for man. It was not for HIM because He already existed, He already had what He needed so everything created, According to Genesis 1 and 2 was a habitat established for the being called human - you and me.

> *Then God said, "Let Us make man in Our image, according to Our likeness; let them have dominion over the fish of the sea, over the birds of the air, and over the cattle, over all the earth and over every creeping thing that creeps on the earth." So God created man in His own image; in the image of God He created him; male and female He created them. Then God blessed them, and God said to them, "Be fruitful and multiply; fill the earth and subdue it; have dominion over the fish of the sea,*

> *over the birds of the air, and over every living thing that moves on the earth."*
>
> *(Genesis 1:26-28).*

If man is the image of God, then man is the physical manifestation of God.

But what did man look like?

> *And the Lord God formed man of the dust of the ground, and breathed into his nostrils the breath of life; and man became a living soul.*
>
> *(Genesis 2:7).*

Here we see the triune nature of man. <u>BODY</u> made from the dust of the ground. GOD's BREATH OF LIFE, which is <u>SPIRIT</u>, because GOD IS SPIRIT. The Hebrew word for Spirit is "Ruach" which is translated as wind or breath. Another word used is *Pneuma* which is an ancient Greek word for "breath" and, in a religious context, for "spirit." And we see <u>SOUL</u>, for man became a Living Soul.

I believe that the breath of God is the spirit of man. Every second of every day you inhale and exhale God, whether you are a believer are not; whether you believe in Jesus or not, you could be an atheist; as a human being, you need God to live; you need God to be alive; alive in the context that a human being is able to move about the earth.

I believe you cannot die spiritually. The Bible says the soul that sins, dies (See Ezekiel 11:20). The Bible says Jesus came to save our souls (See 1 Peter 1:9). We even say in evangelism that we witness to win souls. Which also confirms for me that it is the soul that becomes new when we say yes to Jesus. And it is the soul that dies when we say no.

A dead soul in a human being makes him or her more of an animal, than human. Which is why we see the degradation in our societies. A living soul cannot do some of the things we see people do these days. In today's world, we are dealing with incest, bestiality, sexual brutality and exploitation, abuse and murder of children, corruption, homosexuality; and these are just some the issues that we know about. It is "dead souls" that are capable of this kind of acts. A living soul functions differently, even though there is still a memory of corruption in the body.

What we don't know is how we looked and function as a living soul before the fall, because the suggestion here is that we became dead souls after we sinned. Which means our identity as a living soul is pretty much unknown, even though our souls become new via salvation. Salvation is our rebirth, as a baby. I believe most of us get stuck at the baby stage and very few people have come into maturity because there is a process and, naturally, we much prefer the result than having to go through the process. What we do sometimes is that in order to bypass the process of maturing, we create a false assumption that we have arrived. The process of maturation is mandatory.

Man was also given responsibilities. This is something man (male and female) have a tendency to run from. Even the theory of the rapture is a "I want to get away from responsibility" mentality. The rapture theory is so engrained in many of us that we fail to "occupy until He (Jesus) returns" (See Luke 19:13).

God said to them, "Be fruitful and multiply; fill the earth and subdue it; have dominion over the fish of the sea, over the birds of the air, and over every living thing that moves on the earth."

Fill the earth with what? Why does the earth need to be subdued? Other words for subdue are *pacify, calm, soothe, soften, moderate;* God told man to moderate the affairs of the earth.

Here is the thing: We are responsible for the earth, which means we are the reason the earth is what it is today. We made the mistake of separating ourselves from the world, instead of taking our rightful place in it. We were the ones who should have been the Scientist, Politicians, Business Owners, etc. But we gave it over to the "secular world" while we decided to sit in church waiting for the rapture or death, whichever came first.

Now we are subjected to the rule of non-Christians in the top positions in the world. When we need money, we have to go to non-Christians and become their slaves - to pay for our children's education, to buy food, to use electricity, and basically all the amenities of life because non-Christians control a majority of the resources in the world. Which is why I believe our witness to the world is not very effective because we function below them. We need them in this world more than they need us.

The fall changed us, apparently, but Jesus made it possible for us to be reborn. The suggestion here is that our body is older than our soul, which is why we struggle so much with the flesh and the memory of sin that is in our body, and which is why the Holy Spirit is given to our body (Spirit is poured out on all flesh – See Joel 2:28 | Acts 2:17). The body was made before the soul; the soul died when we sinned; the soul had to be made new via salvation. The real process of Christianity then is for the maturation of our souls, and the transfiguration of our bodies.

So the question I get all the time is, if our real identity is so "God-like" because we were made in the image of God, why don't we see this played out in our daily lives?

In terms of the prophetic, would you give your baby a message to take to your neighbor?

Would you leave your baby in charge of your house?

Would you give your baby your car to drive?

Would you give your baby money to spend?

If God still provides for you indirectly, ensuring all your needs are met and you are taken care of, but He doesn't give you everything you ask for, it means you are still a baby in His house.

A child is born, but a son is given - there is a process.

Which is why I believe that every church needs an effective teaching ministry. We must be equipped to move people through the different stages of the process by teaching revelation and mysteries that will allow their minds to be renewed to greater levels of knowledge and experiences. Our minds are expandable. The entire universe can fit into our minds. God is infinite; He can reveal a new aspect of Himself to you every day for all eternity. Don't get stuck on just one or two revelation - allow it to expand and build upon itself so your soul can grow.

I believe the mandate given to man in Genesis 1 & 2 is still applicable. I believe the end is always the beginning. What we are becoming, is what we were then and what we are now in potential.

We are capable of so much more, and we settle for so little. The fullness of God dwells inside each believer, but your spiritual experiences will always be determined by what you believe to be truth. If you are lacking in spiritual experiences, then you need to re-examine your truth.

I want to make a point using a well-known example and a very controversial topic in our churches today.

Mark 16 says of the believer, you will speak in new tongues, cast out demons, lay hands on the sick and see them recover.

Matthew 10:8 says, you can heal the sick, cleanse the lepers, raise the dead and cast out demons. Freely you have received, freely give.

God says a believer in Christ can raise the dead back to life. You can't say God no longer raises the dead, if you have never tried. And even if you have tried and it didn't happen, you still cannot say God no longer raises the dead. What you need to do is find out why you are unable to do something that God told you explicitly that you can do. Similarly, identity and truth must be determined and accepted by what God said, not by your experiences.

In Christ, you will bear fruit.

In Christ, you will take dominion and rule. Start with your own house, before you try to rule communities, towns, nations.

In Christ, creation is subjected to you. This is a tricky one when your neighbor's dog wants to eat you.

In Christ, you have a new, living soul with unlimited possibilities.

Initiate | Engage | Activate
Meditation Scriptures:

> *Therefore, if anyone is in Christ, he is a new creation; old things have passed away; behold, all things have become new.*
> (2 Corinthians 5:17).
>
> *Do not lie to one another, since you have put off the old man with his deeds, and have put on the new man who is renewed in knowledge according to the image of Him who created him, where there is neither Greek nor Jew, circumcised nor uncircumcised, barbarian, Scythian, slave nor free, but Christ is all and in all.*
> (Colossians 3:9-11).
>
> *Do not remember the former things, nor consider the things of old. Behold, I will do a new thing, now it shall spring forth;*

shall you not know it? I will even make a road in the wilderness and rivers in the desert.
(Isaiah 43:18-19).

Therefore we do not lose heart. Even though our outward man is perishing, yet the inward man is being renewed day by day. For our light affliction, which is but for a moment, is working for us a far more exceeding and eternal weight of glory.
(2 Corinthians 4:16-17).

Then God saw everything that He had made, and indeed it was very good. So the evening and the morning were the sixth day.
(Genesis 1:31).

Through the Lord's mercies we are not consumed, because His compassions fail not. They are new every morning; great is Your faithfulness. "The Lord is my portion," says my soul, "Therefore I hope in Him!"
(Lamentations 3:22-24).

Communion is very vital to us coming into perfection and union with God. When we take the body of Jesus and His blood into our bodies, it causes things to change, unlock and transform. It is the means by which we begin the transfiguration process of our bodies.

The lure of the sin nature by virtue of the memory within the cells of our bodies is very strong. We have heard the stories of great men and women of God who fell to habitual sin. If you have experienced this at all in your walk with the Lord, you know that there is always this pull via temptation to be divided. There are so many Christians today living fragmented lives. On one hand, we try to live the best righteous life that we can, but on the other hand, we practice sin of some sort because we feel like we can't help ourselves when the body calls for it.

> **There are so many Christians today living fragmented lives.**

Communion and the help of the Holy Spirit becomes vital for us to live a whole life, and not be fragmented. We cannot live two or three different versions of ourselves and expect to enjoy the fullness of what God has prepared for us.

If you go to a church that don't practice regular communion, take the practice home. If you live alone, read the appropriate Scriptures, and take communion. If you have a family, make it a part of your daily devotions.

Communion Scriptures:

- 1 Corinthians 10:15-17
- John 6:48-58
- Matthew 26:26-29
- 1 Corinthians 11:23-26

When you intentionally engage with the body and blood of Jesus by regularly partaking in communion, you will activate the kingdom of God that is within you.

CHAPTER THREE

Good and Evil: The Battle Within

I want to start this chapter by examining humanity from the perspective of good and evil. We often associate the term "good" with God, and "evil" with the devil. The consensus is that it is the devil who created evil, when in fact the Bible teaches us that it is man that allowed "evil" to enter the world.

Let's examine this:

> *Now the serpent was more cunning than any beast of the field which the LORD God had made. And he said to the woman, "Has God indeed said, 'You shall not eat of every tree of the garden'?" And the woman said to the serpent, "We may eat the fruit of the trees of the garden; but of*

> *the fruit of the tree which is in the midst of the garden, God has said, 'You shall not eat it, nor shall you touch it, lest you die.'" Then the serpent said to the woman, "You will not surely die. For God knows that in the day you eat of it your eyes will be opened, and you will be like God, knowing good and evil." So when the woman saw that the tree was good for food, that it was pleasant to the eyes, and a tree desirable to make one wise, she took of its fruit and ate. She also gave to her husband with her, and he ate.*
> (Genesis 3:3-6).

Here we see the woman being deceived into disobeying God. The serpent did not pick the fruit (whatever the fruit was) for the woman and hold it to her mouth. He simple talked to her and convince her to disobey God.

> *And Adam was not deceived, but the woman being deceived, fell into transgression.*
> (1 Timothy 2:14).

The enemy's weapon of destruction is deception; that is their power. They can only convince us to do what is not correct, but the choice is ultimately ours. Adam did not have a conversation with the serpent in order to eat as the woman had eaten. He simply choose to partake in whatever consequence she had to face, and he made that decision by having a conversation with himself.

If we should go back even further than this, we see:

> *Then the LORD God took the man and put him in the garden of Eden to tend and keep it. And the LORD God commanded the man, saying, "Of every tree of the garden you may freely eat; but of the tree of the knowledge of good and evil you shall not eat, for in the day that you eat of it you shall surely die."*
> (Genesis 2:15-17).

It was God who made the tree of the knowledge of good and evil and placed it in the garden. We can argue all we want, but we cannot deny Scripture, even if we don't want to agree with what it says:

> *I form the light, and create darkness: I make peace, and create evil: I the* Lord *do all these things.*
>
> (Isaiah 45:7).

I believe that the human being was created predominantly good but with the potential to do evil. The fact that we were created with free will always spoke to the possibility that we could choose to do "life" our own way and walk away from God. We can choose to deny His existence. We can live on our own terms. Note that evil is really a corrupted version of good. Sin is disobedience to God; stepping out of line; using one's will to do what they are not supposed to do. Man is intrinsically good, and intrinsically evil. "The devil made me do it" is a false premise, because we are always seeking someone or something to blame for our bad choices, instead of assuming responsibility for our own actions.

IDENTITY | 45

The process of sonship requires that we assume responsibility for every choice we make and every word we speak, regardless of the results. But there is always a conflict going on within between good and evil. There is no war between God and the devil, because the devil was created by God and can never be equal nor superior to Him. As a matter of fact, when God wanted to put satan in chains, according to the book of revelation, He sent one of the lower ranking angels.

So, how do we deal with this conflict between good and evil within us?

One of the best Biblical examples to look at is Paul:

> *For what I am doing, I do not understand. For what I will to do, that I do not practice; but what I hate, that I do. If, then, I do what I will not to do, I agree with the law that it is good. But now, it is no longer I who do it, but sin that dwells in me. For I know that in me*

> *(that is, in my flesh) nothing good dwells; for to will is present with me, but how to perform what is good I do not find. For the good that I will to do, I do not do; but the evil I will not to do, that I practice. Now if I do what I will not to do, it is no longer I who do it, but sin that dwells in me. I find then a law, that evil is present with me, the one who wills to do good. For I delight in the law of God according to the inward man. But I see another law in my members, warring against the law of my mind, and bringing me into captivity to the law of sin which is in my members. O wretched man that I am! Who will deliver me from this body of death?*
>
> (Romans 7:15-24).

Here we see confirmation that the record or memory of sin and evil is in the body. The soul is good and new, but the body maintains the record of corruption, which is why both are always in conflict. Paul referred to the source of evil as this "body of death." This struggle is inward, and evil can only be overcome with good.

> *Do not be overcome by evil but overcome evil with good.*
> (Romans 12:21).

Almost every decision we face in life will almost always be based on the merit of good or evil. There is nothing wrong with eating fruit from a tree, but if God says not to, we should not. But the tree was not created just to tempt us. There will come a time when we can eat from the tree, but only when we are ready. If we partake too soon, we cripple the process and hamper the full effect that it is supposed to have. We can use sex as an example. Our libido gets turned on quite early in life and our hormones are raging, but we are told we cannot partake of it until marriage. The question is, what do we do with all these hormones while we wait for that glorious day?

The tree of the knowledge of good and evil may have been meant to be eaten from, but not before the right time. Sex is a powerful energetic force that can create a baby, so it is possibly our creative energy that may be the driving force we need in our younger days to achieve great things. Notice that it is at its highest peak during the times when we are usually pursuing our career and seeking to become an agent of change in the world. It could be possible that that energetic force was given to drive us passionately through that stage of our life in order to make something great of ourselves, instead of being just a source of pleasure. Partaking of it too early can bring unwanted complications to one's life. Which also means that partaking of sexual intercourse and expelling that energy too soon may be the reason we cripple our creative power and hamper our ability to create anything of lasting value or make something of ourselves.

The war between good and evil is intrinsic. The greatest battle we will ever face in this life is within ourselves. The only being who has the power to hinder your emergence as a manifested son of God is you. External influences only seek to distract us from the real battle, which is why most of us live a defeated life, even when we think we have the enemy under our feet. The real enemy is you.

> **The only being who has the power to hinder your emergence as a manifested son of God is you.**

Initiate | Engage | Activate
Meditation Scriptures:

Do not be overcome by evil, but overcome evil with good.

(Romans 12:21).

Do not be deceived; evil companionships corrupt good habits.

(1 Corinthians 15:33).

Who will render to each according to his works; indeed to those who with patience in good work are seeking for glory, and

honor, and incorruptibility, everlasting life. But to those who indeed disobeying the truth out of self-seeking, and obeying unrighteousness, will be anger and wrath.
(Romans 2:6-8).

Depart from evil and do good; and live forevermore.
(Psalm 37:27).

Let no one being tempted say, I am tempted from God. For God is not tempted by evils, and He tempts no one. But each one is tempted by his lusts, being drawn away and seduced by them. Then when lust has conceived, it brings forth sin. And sin, when it is fully formed, brings forth death.
(James 1:13-15).

I say, then, walk in the Spirit and you shall not fulfill the lusts of the flesh. For the flesh lusts against the Spirit, and the Spirit against the flesh. And these are contrary to one another; lest whatever you may will, these things you do.
(Galatians 5:16-17).

IDENTITY | 51

> *Depart from evil and do good; seek peace and pursue it.*
>
> (Psalm 34:14).
>
> *The eyes of Jehovah are in every place, beholding the evil and the good.*
>
> (Proverbs 15:3).

If you can reserve one hour out of each day to practice the principles in this book, it can change your life. What I want to encourage you to do is sit with yourself, alone, and remove all distractions; turn off the cell phone. You want to pay attention to your thoughts; don't try to control them yet, just let them come. As each thought enters your mind, examine it on the merit of good and evil and try to determine which category it fits in. What you deem to be evil thoughts, erase it from your mind; intentionally force yourself not to think that thought after you have examined it. Whatever is good, process that and keep it. Meditate on the good thoughts and see if there is additional revelation there to be unlocked. This is also a good practice to learn to hear God's voice; the Spirit of God is always speaking.

There are many voices that speak and many sources that can project thoughts and images into your mind. The challenge is to know what to keep and what to discard as these thoughts influence what you say and what you do. Your body has a voice; so does your mind. There is also a record of the previous generation going back many centuries that also has a voice. Your blood carries a lot of memories, which is why a lot of Christians engage in generational warfare; which is why you find yourself struggling with a lot of the problems your predecessors had. Their voice also speaks. But this is important for the next topic that we will be discussing.

CHAPTER FOUR

Redeeming The Imagination: Renewing Our Minds

Paul makes it clear In Romans 12 that the process of transformation involves renewing the mind. Most believers don't know what this is or what it looks like, but it is a process that we see played out in one's development.

If we should consider the process we go through to learn, we realize that the school system is designed to always teach us at a higher level than where we are. This process moves us through kindergarten all the way through university and beyond. The technology of growth is to expose the mind to new information in order for it to expand. The more you learn, the more you can learn.

There is a renewing of the mind that actually takes place in the educational process. Something similar is needed in order for the soul to grow.

There are two human faculties that get engaged when one is learning, and that is the imagination and the mind. Both are expandable and can hold unlimited amount of knowledge, even more knowledge than we can assimilate in our entire earthly lives. Knowledge is important in growth.

> *I beseech you therefore, brethren, by the mercies of God, that you present your bodies a living sacrifice, holy, acceptable to God, which is your reasonable service. And do not be conformed to this world, but be transformed by the renewing of your mind, that you may prove what is that good and acceptable and perfect will of God.*
>
> (Romans 12:1-2).

There are two very powerful commands in this Scripture:

1. Present your body to God as a living sacrifice.
2. Be transformed by renewing your mind.

The renewing of the mind can provide the strength that is needed to present your body to God, which I believe this generation is finding hard to do. A lot of effort should be placed in this area because your body has great value to its Creator, which is why He became human to redeem you. Scant regard is given to the body by believers because there is word on the streets that we will be getting a new one, but the new body is actually a transfigured or glorified version of the old. How do I know this? Look at Jesus and Moses. They both have their original bodies, but it is glorified, or we could use the church phrase, "fully redeemed."

The pre-cursor to a redeemed body is a renewed mind and a sanctified imagination.

Why is the imagination important? I believe it is the window into the spiritual world. The imagination can be used to see. For people who don't have the natural gift of spiritual sight and insight, I usually tell them to pay attention to their dreams, imagination and what comes into the mind. We interact with the invisible world every day and night; and it interacts with us perpetually. Angels encamp around us (See Psalm 34:7); there are the clouds of witnesses (See Hebrews 12:1), men in white linen (See Daniel 12:7), numerous angelic structures (See Hebrews 13:2), spirits of just men made perfect (See Hebrews 12:23), etc. We are never alone. God is always in us, by us and with us.

The imagination is very useful in your growing up into sonship.

Renewing of the mind is vital. Why is this?

> *For as he thinks in his heart, so is he.*
> (Proverbs 23:7a).

IDENTITY | 57

There is a suggestion here that a man thinks with his heart. If the mind to be renewed is in the heart, it makes sense that pure thoughts equals a pure heart, therefore, according to Matthew 5:8, our spiritual eyes will pop open to see God.

If the Bible is truth, your thoughts create your reality, which is why knowledge is so vital to your growth. The more you know, the more you are able to assimilate, and the more you are able to do. Look at some of the technologies, buildings, devices and inventions that came out of the mind of man. It is also important what you know and what you choose to think about:

> *Finally, brethren, whatever things are true, whatever things are noble, whatever things are just, whatever things are pure, whatever things are lovely, whatever things are of good report, if there is any virtue and if there is anything praiseworthy—meditate on these things. The things which you learned and received*

> *and heard and saw in me, these do, and the God of peace will be with you.*
> (Philippians 4:8-9).

Your thoughts is your responsibility. God designed it that way. Paul confirmed it in his writing. There is no point in believing otherwise. You must guard what you process in your mind. Let the wrong information in, and it can stunt your life; let the right information in, and you can be transformed and also become an agent of transformation.

> **Your thoughts is your responsibility.**

> *For though we walk in the flesh, we do not war according to the flesh. For the weapons of our warfare are not carnal but mighty in God for pulling down strongholds, casting down arguments and every high thing that exalts itself against the knowledge of God, bringing every thought into captivity to the obedience of Christ,*

> *and being ready to punish all disobedience when your obedience is fulfilled.*
> (2 Corinthians 10:3-6).

Strongholds, arguments, every high thing that exalts itself against the knowledge of God are all internal; none of these are external. The real spiritual battle that we fight is within.

The fall in the Garden of Eden took place because a wrong thought was processed and acted upon.

Lao Tzu penned these words:

> Watch your thoughts, they become your words; watch your words, they become your actions; watch your actions, they become your habits; watch your habits, they become your character; watch your character, it becomes your destiny.

The thought that becomes your reality is a stronghold, and strongholds make people think that is the way they are and they cannot change. Anyone can change. Anyone can become someone less or someone greater. It begins as a thought. I could tell you to think God-sized thoughts, but you would probably quote this text:

> *"For My thoughts are not your thoughts, nor are your ways My ways," says the Lord. "For as the heavens are higher than the earth, so are My ways higher than your ways, and My thoughts than your thoughts."*
>
> (Isaiah 55:8-9).

What is amazing is that Paul now says:

> For *"who has known the mind of the Lord that he may instruct Him?"* But we have the mind of Christ.
>
> (1 Corinthians 2:16).

Did our mind become the mind of Christ at conversion or do we have two minds at work within our being?

That is a good question.

One thing I do know; a conversation takes place within us before each decision is made. That is just the way we are. We may not even be aware of the conversation, but no one just acts arbitrary. We reason before we decide, so our decisions can change if we change our reasoning capacity, and reasoning has to do with the mind.

The mind of man is a powerful thing and reality as we know it flows out of the mind. Everything we use, every building, every invention, everything we see that was not a part of natural creation was once a thought inside the mind of a man. That is how powerful your mind is, so Paul's suggestion that we pay close attention to it and seek to renew it in order to come into conformity with the image and likeness of God is commendable. It is impossible to step into a new season or comprehend the "new thing" that God wants to do in you unless the mind is renewed.

While we need to be careful of the thoughts we inevitably process in our minds, we must remain open to receive information, revelation and insight. We don't know everything, but the mind of the One who does know everything is inside of us; we have the mind of Christ. That is why you can hear a revelation that is completely new to you, but somehow you resonate with it.

Our minds give us access to mysteries and the unknown. Our minds can change our reality. Our minds are so powerful, that Paul says it needs renewal. Anything that is released from heaven to the earth must first pass through the mind of man, which suggests that the mind is a gateway between the heavenly and earthly realms. In essence, we can stop something from coming through from there to here or we can allow it.

Finally, the mind and imagination are vital in the initial stages of ascension. If we are already in heaven, then we must practice being raptured; and going to and fro, taking what is there (in heaven) and bringing it here (on earth). Is all that really possible?

> *Jesus replied, "Truly I tell you, the Son is not able to do anything on his own, but only what he sees the Father doing. For whatever the Father does, the Son likewise does these things."*
> (John 5:19).

If we are going to mature into sonship, we must learn to see what the Father is doing so we can do likewise. This is where relationship is crucial, and it starts in the mind.

Practice to ascend; go into heaven using the Word and your imagination. Expose your imagination to the glory and splendor of heaven and the light and presence of God, and it will sanctify your imagination. You will see differently. Ideas and creative inventions will come. Life changing technologies, business ideas, etc. will come. Our imagination and our minds can be used for evil and it can be used for good.

Your imagination is not evil continually. God gave it to you for a purpose. It was built into man.

Your mind is a spiritual technology for change and transformation. Think back to the beginning. God brought all the animals to Adam for him to name them. In naming them, Adam also solidified their nature. How was he able to do that? I believe both his mind and imagination was engaged in the process. How you think determines how you function. What you think will eventually become your reality.

> **How you think determines how you function. What you think will eventually become your reality.**

Initiate | Engage | Activate
Meditation Scriptures:

And the Lord said, Behold, the people is one, and they have all one language; and this they begin to do: and now nothing will be restrained from them, which they have imagined to do.

(Genesis 11:6).

Keep your heart with all diligence; for out of it are the issues of life.

(Proverbs 4:23).

A good man out of the good treasure of his heart brings forth the good. And an evil man out of the evil treasure of his heart brings forth the evil. For out of the abundance of the heart his mouth speaks.

(Luke 6:45).

Then hear in Heaven Your dwelling-place, and forgive, and do, and give to every man according to all his ways, whose heart You know. For You, You only, know the hearts of all the sons of Adam.

(1 Kings 8:39).

And you, Solomon my son, know the God of your father and serve Him with a perfect heart and with a willing mind. For Jehovah searches all hearts and understands all the imaginations of the thoughts. If you seek Him, He will be found by you. But if you forsake Him, He will cast you off forever.

(1 Chronicles 28:9).

> *But Jehovah said to Samuel, do not look on his face, nor on his height, because I have refused him. For He does not see as man sees. For man looks on the outward appearance, but Jehovah looks on the heart.*
> (1 Samuel 16:7).
>
> *Let the words of my mouth and the meditation of my heart be pleasing in Your sight, O Jehovah, my Rock and my Redeemer.*
> (Psalm 19:14).
>
> *Examine me, O Jehovah, and prove me; purify my heart and my mind.*
> (Psalm 26:2).
>
> *Shall not God search this out? For He knows the secrets of the heart.*
> (Psalm 44:21).

At this stage in your journey, it is good to keep a journal. Write down the revelations you may receive while meditating. If you see an image, write a description of it. You also want to start recording your dreams and any visions you may be having. If you have been diligent in applying the principles in this book, by now you may be noticing some changes. If not, keep on persevering until the kingdom of God opens up to you.

Another great way to exercise your mind and imagination is by sitting quietly and ask Holy Spirit to show you something. Wait, and pay keen attention to the images, etc. that are projected in your mind. You may even see the face of someone you need to pray for or call and encourage; and you may even see something happening that you are not aware of. It could be a moment in the past or future. Document these occurrences for future reference.

You can also use Scripture to engage the imagination. A good place to start is revelation and Ezekiel. Try to see what these writers were trying to describe. Don't try to understand what they are saying, just try to see it.

CHAPTER FIVE

All Things Are Yours: But You Need To Grow Up

Maturity does not happen overnight. I am always fascinated by the potential of human beings to grow from a baby into a responsible, pleasure seeking, intellectual, emotional, literate adult. The adult version of you was sitting inside you as a baby, in potential. It is the same way that I believe the glorious being we are pre-destined to become is also now sitting inside the adult. We are learning beings, with a unique DNA strand that opens at the top and bottom, meaning we can become far more than we already are at any given stage of our life. While I could steer this argument in the direction of our professions, or even social influence, I want to focus on our emergence as sons of God bearing the responsibility that accompanies that position.

Every aspect of our lives play a significant role in our maturing, in our becoming. But there are some essential components that we cannot overlook that is needed in the process. The first being, "Faith." You needed faith to take you to where you are now, and you are going to need that same faith to take you all the way, so when we talk about all things being yours, for this to be true, as the Bible states, you must first believe it.

> *So Jesus answered and said to them, "Have faith in God. For assuredly, I say to you, whoever says to this mountain, 'Be removed and be cast into the sea,' and does not doubt in his heart, but believes that those things he says will be done, he will have whatever he says. Therefore I say to you, whatever things you ask when you pray, believe that you receive them, and you will have them.*
>
> (Mark 11:22-24).

This is a big statement that defies our reality because most of us have a mountain in our lives that needs moving. We may have even spoken to it many times before and it has not budged. How are we to believe what God says when our experience dictates that it could not be true? Maybe Jesus was not being literal. Maybe it was a symbolic statement. Maybe those words do not apply to us in this dispensation. The fact is, it was Jesus who said, not one of His disciples, which makes it hard to argue with the statement. Somehow, it must be true. But Jesus did not stop there:

> *"Most assuredly, I say to you, he who believes in Me, the works that I do he will do also; and greater works than these he will do, because I go to My Father. And whatever you ask in My name, that I will do, that the Father may be glorified in the Son. If you ask anything in My name, I will do it.*
>
> *(John 14:12-14).*

This is an even bigger statement. Whatever you ask for, in His Name, He WILL do it. And Jesus even attaches the glory of God to this promise, which means that God is glorified in answered prayers. When was the last time you saw the glory of God?

In addition to these promises, Paul now says:

> *Therefore let no one boast in men. For <u>all things are yours</u>: whether Paul or Apollos or Cephas, or the world or life or death, or things present or things to come—all are yours. And you are Christ's, and Christ is God's.*
>
> (1 Corinthians 3:21-23).

So that thing you are asking for, and think you are not getting for whatever reason you think God may have to withhold it from you is yours; it is all yours. I became fascinated by the use of the word "all things" so I had to look it up. Do you know what it means? It means "all things"; nothing is left out; it all belongs to you. Now, I did not say it; God did.

The best posture we can have when contemplating these things is one of faith. We must know, with no shadow of a doubt, that all things are possible, and all things are ours.

> Jesus said to him, "If you can believe, all things are possible to him who believes."
> (Mark 9:23).

I like this particular text because it never said, "…to him who believes in God." Belief, on any level, can pull what you need from one realm into this one. You can experience manifestation on the merit of your belief alone, without even cementing your faith in Jesus Christ. Why do you think non-believers are able to do even greater and more impossible things than we could ever imagine? They did it, because they believed they could. And if belief alone can put a airplane 30,000 feet in the sky for hours; make a multi-billion dollar business out of fry chicken; build skyscrapers, weapons of mass destruction, and a device so small that it can hold in your pocket; a device that eliminated communication barriers and made people thousands of miles away our next door neighbor; what can belief in Jesus accomplish? Do you get the point?

I like Jesus' take on the matter:

> *Later He appeared to the eleven as they sat at the table; and He rebuked their unbelief and hardness of heart, because they did not believe those who had seen Him after He had risen. And He said to them, "Go into all the world and preach the gospel to every creature. He who believes and is baptized will be saved; but he who does not believe will be condemned. And these signs will follow those who believe: In My name they will cast out demons; they will speak with new tongues; they will take up serpents; and if they drink anything deadly, it will by no means hurt them; they will lay hands on the sick, and they will recover." So then, after the Lord had spoken to them, He was received up into heaven, and sat down at the right hand of God. And they went out and preached*

> *everywhere, the Lord working with them and confirming the word through the accompanying signs. Amen.*
> (Mark 16:14-20).

Do you see what a believer in Christ can do?

1. Cast out demons.
2. Speak with new tongues.
3. Take up serpents.
4. Not be hurt by anything deadly.
5. Lay hands on the sick and see them recover.

These are the basic elementary doctrines of Christ. This is baby stuff. There are greater levels and dimensions awaiting those who come into maturity (See Hebrews 5 & 6).

Faith is the starting point, and faith opens up the realms of the impossible for you. Faith gives you access to unlimited resources and power. Faith is your foot in the door, but don't get stuck standing in the doorway. Enter into God and go after His heart and there will come a day when you will see God face to face and then you will no longer need faith, but until then; faith is the greatest technology that you have been given as a child of God.

> *But without faith it is impossible to please Him, for he who comes to God must believe that He is, and that He is a rewarder of those who diligently seek Him.*
> (Hebrews 11:6).

In Christ, you have everything to gain, and nothing to lose. This is your legacy, your inheritance. You were not made for sin and a mediocre existence; God spoke creation into existence, but when it came to humanity, He took a more personal and direct approach. He fashioned man with His own hands and put His breathe (His life) into man, forming a living being; a living soul. Even King David says you were knitted in your mother's womb (See Psalm 139:13). You are not a mistake. You were born for this. You are unique and authentic, and there is no replica of you in the entire universe. You are one of a kind, and God sees you.

Nothing gives the Father more pleasure than to watch you grow in grace. As you mature, He releases greater responsibility to you in His house. It belongs to you anyway. He doesn't condemn you for falling when you try to walk, nor does He expect you to be perfect. God has written you in His will as a co-heir of His estate, but you need to grow up. Don't get stuck and don't allow yourself to remain a baby in God's house forever. Dive headlong into the process so God can initiate the maturation of your soul. Study the Scriptures and thoughts presented here and keep your mind open to receive even greater revelations than what I have shared with you. This is only the beginning of your journey.

> *But as it is written: "Eye has not seen, nor ear heard, nor have entered into the heart of man the things which God has prepared for those who love Him."*
> (1 Corinthians 2:9)

Everything we have talked about to this point has been seen, heard and thought about. It has also been written, so this is not it. There is more. God has much, much more than this for you. This just introduces you to the process, but the choice to go in is entirely yours.

> *I am the door. If anyone enters by Me, he will be saved, and will go in and out and find pasture.*
>
> (John 10:9).

Enter through Jesus Christ. Engage the Holy Spirit in the process. Please don't try to bypass a relationship with God to get in. As you position yourself in God, in Christ, layer by layer, level by level, dimension by dimension, the fullness of Christ and who you are in Him will become for you an unfolding revelation and a lifestyle.

Initiate | Engage | Activate Meditation Scriptures:

> *I waited patiently for the Lord; And He inclined to me, and heard my cry.*
>
> (Psalm 40:1).

Behold the proud, His soul is not upright in him; But the just shall live by his faith.
(Habakkuk 2:4).

Now if God so clothes the grass of the field, which today is, and tomorrow is thrown into the oven, will He not much more clothe you, O you of little faith?
(Matthew 6:30).

But Jesus turned around, and when He saw her He said, "Be of good cheer, daughter; your faith has made you well." And the woman was made well from that hour.
(Matthew 9:22).

Then He touched their eyes, saying, "According to your faith let it be to you."
(Matthew 9:29).

Then Jesus answered and said to her, "O woman, great is your faith! Let it be to you as you desire." And her daughter was healed from that very hour.
(Matthew 15:28).

Now in the fourth watch of the night Jesus went to them, walking on the sea. And when the disciples saw Him walking on the sea, they were troubled, saying, "It is a ghost!" And they cried out for fear. But immediately Jesus spoke to them, saying, "Be of good cheer! It is I; do not be afraid." And Peter answered Him and said, "Lord, if it is You, command me to come to You on the water." So He said, "Come." And when Peter had come down out of the boat, he walked on the water to go to Jesus. But when he saw that the wind was boisterous, he was afraid; and beginning to sink he cried out, saying, "Lord, save me!" And immediately Jesus stretched out His hand and caught him, and said to him, "O you of little faith, why did you doubt?"

(Matthew 14:25-31)

So Jesus said to them, "Because of your unbelief; for assuredly, I say to you, if you have faith as a mustard seed, you will say to this mountain, 'Move from here to there,' and it will move; and nothing will be impossible for you."

(Matthew 17:20).

So Jesus answered and said to them, "Assuredly, I say to you, if you have faith and do not doubt, you will not only do what was done to the fig tree, but also if you say to this mountain, 'Be removed and be cast into the sea,' it will be done."

(Matthew 21:21).

So Jesus answered and said to them, "Have faith in God."

(Mark 11:22).

So the Lord said, "If you have faith as a mustard seed, you can say to this mulberry tree, 'Be pulled up by the roots and be planted in the sea,' and it would obey you."

(Luke 17:6).

I tell you that He will avenge them speedily. Nevertheless, when the Son of Man comes, will He really find faith on the earth?

(Luke 18:8).

> *And His name, through faith in His name, has made this man strong, whom you see and know. Yes, the faith which comes through Him has given him this perfect soundness in the presence of you all.*
>
> (Acts 3:16).
>
> *And Stephen, full of faith and power, did great wonders and signs among the people.*
>
> (Acts 6:8).
>
> *First, I thank my God through Jesus Christ for you all, that your faith is spoken of throughout the whole world.*
>
> (Romans 1:8).
>
> *For I am not ashamed of the gospel of Christ, for it is the power of God to salvation for everyone who believes, for the Jew first and also for the Greek.*
>
> (Romans 1:16).
>
> *So then faith comes by hearing, and hearing by the word of God.*
>
> (Romans 10:17).

That your faith should not be in the wisdom of men but in the power of God.
(1 Corinthians 2:5).

And now abide faith, hope, love, these three; but the greatest of these is love.
(1 Corinthians 13:13).

Let no one despise your youth, but be an example to the believers in word, in conduct, in love, in spirit, in faith, in purity.
(1 Timothy 4:12).

Therefore we also, since we are surrounded by so great a cloud of witnesses, let us lay aside every weight, and the sin which so easily ensnares us, and let us run with endurance the race that is set before us, looking unto Jesus, the author and finisher of our faith, who for the joy that was set before Him endured the cross, despising the shame, and has sat down at the right hand of the throne of God.
(Hebrews 12:1).

The challenge for us, as we bring this book to a close, is to go and practice faith. I cannot determine a timeline for you as to how long you need to practice before you experience manifestation. Manifestation will flow more out of a developing relationship with God, than applying formulas.

It is my prayer that your faith begins to produce immediately, but I am genuinely unable to guarantee it. Todd White prayed for thousands of people before he saw his first miracle. Praying Medic, whom I have met personally, prayed for hundreds before he saw his first miracle.

> **Manifestation will flow more out of a developing relationship with God, than applying formulas.**

In practicing faith, we bring light to this world, but we must never use signs, wonders and miracles to affirm our character. While it is good to walk in the power of the Holy Spirit, it is better to be known by God and live righteously; as much as it is in our power to do. It always boils down to relationship because love is better than power; Love is the true, real, authentic power. You can have power but no love; but you cannot have love and no power.

Pray for people who are sick. Don't be afraid to do this. Offer to pray if they tell you they are not feeling well. If you visit a hospital, offer prayer. Lay hands and believe God and don't stop until you start seeing results. You may be the only hope someone who is terribly sick has. Encourage the sick and oppressed to believe God, even if their situation does not change. It is better to die with faith in your heart, than live in fear. If you are up to it, don't be afraid to speak life to someone who has died. You carry within you the resurrected power of Jesus Christ. The same Spirit who rose Christ from the dead lives in you. If you only believe, you can raise the dead, heal the sick, cast out demons, etc.

> **It is better to die with faith in your heart, than live in fear.**

Practice the presence of God. Intentionally be aware of His presence in your life at all times, regardless of what you are engaged in at the moment. We need to step away from the mentality that God can only be experienced at "church." Wherever you are, at any given moment of the day or night, God is there, and you are a carrier of His presence. Spend time to stir up the presence within through awareness, worship and prayer. Your prayer doesn't need to be audible; it can just be a whisper of the heart. Practice contemplative prayer where you sit and talk to God from within. You don't always need to be vocal because God's ear is always tuned to the frequency of your heart. He hears your thoughts, so your thoughts are, in fact, prayers.

> God's ear is always tuned to the frequency of your heart.

Finally, demonstrate your love for God by loving people. Don't just love the people you like, but show love to those you find intolerable and unlovable. Practice forgiveness. Don't wait too long to release people who have offended you. Keep very short records as it relates to this.

Give to the poor. Don't concern yourself with what they will or will not do with what you give to them. Our responsibility is to give. If they make bad choices with the gift they have received, it is on them. We also make bad choices with the gifts God gives, but He keeps on giving.

> Love is the light that we have the power to bring to this world.

Love is the light that we have the power to bring to this world. God is love, so the one who becomes love, becomes like God; made in His image and likeness.

Conclusion

I pray and hope that this book has challenged and shifted your perception. The goal was for you to see yourself through God's eyes, to understand that you are His idea and it is His identity and not your own concocted version of yourself that truly matters.

When man fell, our soul died, and our consciousness shattered. Initially, we were so aware of the spiritual dimension that Adam could hear the voice of God walking in the garden. We lost that. But Jesus came to restore all that was lost, but He also left us with the responsibility to work it out in our individual lives.

> *Therefore, my beloved, as you have always obeyed, not as in my presence only, but now much more in my absence, work out your*

> *own salvation with fear and trembling; for it is God who works in you both to will and to do for His good pleasure.*
> (Philippians 2:12-13).

Do not make your relationship with God the responsibility of others; it is yours and yours alone. God has given you all things, but you must assimilate it by first gaining the knowledge of who you are and what you have been given, and then learn how to come into the fullness of your inheritance.

We must conform, we must be transformed, we must be changed. Growth suggest non-passivity and non-stagnation. We must never allow ourselves to get stuck at any level, no matter how sweet and mind-blowing it is. Salvation is free, but work is still involved. You studied hard and practiced relentlessly to achieve a career; do the same for your spiritual life.

Your Identity in Christ was Restored through the blood and body of Jesus Christ. Your

Identity is Revealed through the revelations that keep coming from heaven to earth. It is time for you to Initiate so your authentic Identity becomes your reality.

Connect With Me

Facebook:
authorcorvillemcleish

Instagram:
cleveland.mcleish

Website:
www.christianplaywright.org

email: info@hcpbookpublishing.com

Whatssap:
1-876-352-2650